SHANGHAI
上 海

FOREIGN LANGUAGES PRESS   BEIJING

外文出版社　北京

SHANGHAI

Shanghai, with a population of more than 13 million, is the largest city in China. It is often likened to a dazzling pearl in the center of the east coast, where the golden channel of the Yangtze River flows to the sea.

Long and Colorful Past　Shanghai has a long and colorful history, dating as far back as the third century B.C. By the Song Dynasty (960-1279) it had developed into a burgeoning commercial harbor, and in the Ming Dynasty (1368-1644) it became China's largest cotton textile center, with a flourishing commercial economy. In 1685 (the 24th year of Emperor Kangxi's reign) the Qing government set up a customs office in Shanghai, as the city was by then a busy hub of coastal shipping, and was also connected with China's inland areas via the navigation routes along the Yangtze.

In 1840 the Opium War broke out between China and Britain, and in 1843 Shanghai was forced by colonialists to open as a commercial port to foreign powers. Several countries set up concessions (which were virtually "countries within a country") there. The 1.5-km belt along the Huangpu River between the Waibaidu Bridge and Yan'an Donglu was called Waitan Bund. Here buildings in distinct foreign styles, which are still used, once housed foreign consulates, banks, commercial firms and newspaper offices. From then on Shanghai was an important port through which the imperialist powers poured their goods and through which they plundered China's raw materials and wealth. Shanghai thus became a "paradise for adventurers." Meanwhile, the national industries, such as the light, textile and processing industries, found it difficult to survive as foreign entrepreneurs dominated the markets. Many Chinese thinkers, revolutionaries and writers in Shanghai called on the people to resist this encroachment, and took an active part in various kinds of struggles for national rights and liberation. If Waitan can be taken as a microcosm of Shanghai under the rule of colonialism, then the former residence and memorial hall of Lu Xun, the former residence of Dr. Sun Yat-sen, the former residence of Soong Ching Ling and the site of the First National Congress of the Communist Party of China are symbols of the unyielding spirit of resistance of the Chinese people.

Shanghai grew in a lopsided way. But over nearly half a century since the founding of the People's Republic the Chinese government has made great efforts to rebuild Shanghai into a metropolis renowned both throughout China and abroad. Now, it has become the largest port for foreign trade and one of the largest industrial bases, as well as a center of finance, science and technology, culture and trade, in China.

Shoppers' Paradise   Shanghai was founded on commerce. And still today the east China metropolis is well known for its shops stocked with goods of every kind, of excellent quality and serviced with expertise and courtesy. Nanjing Road, Huaihai Road and the old Chenghuangmiao (City God Temple) shopping market are ideal shopping areas. Nanjing and Huaihai roads are lined with imposing commercial buildings and renowned traditional shops, where crowds of people from all over China and the rest of the world as well mingle as they browse among the stalls. The Chenghuangmiao market is still filled with small shops, dealing mainly in local specialties. To wander through the crowded alleys and lanes in the market is to experience the very heartbeat of Shanghai — the dynamism of commerce.

Downtown Cultural Relics and Scenic Spots   Though Shanghai is a prosperous metropolis which is densely populated, there are many places for rest and relaxation downtown. For instance, the Yuyuan Garden built in the south China garden style of the Ming and Qing dynasties receives more than 10,000 visitors every day, on average. The Jade Buddha Temple, a leading Buddhist place of worship in south China, lies on Anyuan Road in the Putuo District. The white jade statue of Buddha located in the Recumbent Buddha Hall and the jade seated Buddha in the Jade Buddha Building in the temple were brought there many years ago from Myanmar. On the outskirts and in the outer suburbs of Shanghai one sees typical south China villages along streams and rivers. The most famous scenic spots are the Longhua Pagoda and Longhua Temple, the Garden of Grand View Resort beside Dianshan Lake, the Guyi Park and Qiuxiapu Garden at Jiading, the Zuibai Pool and the Fangta Garden at Songjiang, and the Catholic cathedral on Sheshan Hill.

Charm of Life in the Old Lanes　Though in recent years residential districts with complete living facilities have mushroomed in Shanghai, many Shanghainese are still sentimentally attached to the life in Shanghai's old-fashioned houses located typically in narrow, winding lanes.

The resourceful people of Shanghai have a reputation for being canny and thrifty. We can see this especially in their daily lives. Every morning, housewives go to the markets carrying baskets, wander among the vegetable and fruit stalls and butcher's shops, bargaining and comparing, and then return with their baskets full of fresh vegetables, tender meat and live fish and shrimps, which are the result of hard and skillful bargaining.

Shanghai people not only have the courage to absorb and learn what they need from foreign culture, they also love Chinese traditions and culture. For instance, early every morning people both young and old meet to engage in modern vigorous dancing and exercising in parks and squares, which is a venerated custom in China. Traditional operas and performances, such as Beijing, Kunqu, Shaoxing and Shanghai operas, and story telling and ballad singing in the Suzhou dialect are all popular among the Shanghainese. At the Longhua Temple Fair, which takes place in April (the third month by the lunar calendar), a wide variety of snacks with indigenous flavors as well as excellent handicrafts are on sale, and acrobatics and Chinese martial arts are performed for the public. All this shows that traditional culture is alive and well in the hearts of Shanghai's people.

Shanghai in the Coming Century　With the opening of the 1990s, the Chinese government proclaimed to the world its strategic decision to develop the wasteland of Pudong (lit. "east of the Huangpu River"). The New Pudong District, with an area of 522 sq km, is separated from the main urban district by the Huangpu River. Taking advantage of the development and opening of Pudong, Shanghai has entered a new stage in its reform and opening to the outside world. As a result, great changes have taken place in the metropolis in recent years, as a batch of infrastructural facilities have sprung up in the New Pudong District, including the Nanpu and Yangpu bridges, the tunnel across the Huangpu River, a new port and power plants. The Lujiazui financial and commercial district, Waigaoqiao Free Trade Area, Jinqiao Export Processing Zone and Zhangjiang Hi-Tech Park are now basically ready to receive foreign investors. Experts predict that the development of Pudong is of great significance for and will exert a tremendous influence on the development of Shanghai as well as the drive for the further reform and opening and the economic take-off of the Yangtze Delta and the entire country. In the next century Pudong will become a major center of finance, commerce, real estate trading, information, and material supplies.

上　海

　　上海是中国最大的一座城市,拥有 1300 余万人口。它位于中国东部南北海岸线的中心,是黄金水道长江入海处的一颗明珠。

　　回眸看上海　　上海的历史也堪称久远而多彩。公元前三世纪已有文字记载,到了宋代(公元 960 - 1279 年)上海开始成为一个新兴的贸易港口,明代(公元 1368 - 1644 年)发展为最大的棉纺业中心,商业经济日趋发达。清康熙二十四年(1685 年),清政府在上海设海关,上海逐渐成为"江海之通津,东南之都会"。

　　1840 年爆发了中英鸦片战争。1843 年上海被殖民主义者强迫开辟为通商口岸。一些国家纷纷到上海抢占地盘,设立租界,成为"国中之国"。黄浦江畔从外白渡桥到延安东路约 1.5 公里的地段被称之为外滩。马路一侧一幢幢具有不同风格的高楼大厦,就是当年这些国家设立的领事馆、银行、总会、商行、报社等。之后的一百多年里,上海成了外国殖民主义者在中国倾销商品,掠夺原料、财富的重要口岸。上海成为"冒险家的乐园"。与此同时,中国的民族产业如轻工、纺织、加工业等在夹缝中苦苦挣扎。各种势力在这里碰撞、较量。许多思想家、革命者、文学家为争国权、为民族解放在大上海呼唤、呐喊,积极展开各种斗争。如果说外滩的外国建筑群是殖民主义统治下上海的缩影,那么鲁迅故居与纪念馆、孙中山故居、宋庆龄故居、中国共产党第一次代表大会会址等等则是中国人民不屈的反抗精神的象征。

　　旧上海是一个畸形发展的城市。近半个世纪以来,中国政府对上海进行了艰巨的改造和建设,使上海成为闻名海内外的大都市。它是中国最大的对外贸易港口和最大的工业基地之一,也是重要的金融、科技、文化和贸易中心。

　　购物天堂　　上海的商业历史悠久,素以店多面广、品种齐全、质量上乘、服务优良而著称。南京路、淮海路、老城隍庙商场是人们理想的购物场所。南京路、淮海路上聚集着享誉全国的老商号和现代化商厦，外地人、本地人都慕名来此购物，常年人潮涌动。老城隍庙则是一个小商品市场集中的地方，具有小（小商店）、土（土特产）、特（特色商品）、多（多品种规格）的特色。徘徊在拥挤的小街上，穿梭于小商店间，既能体察上海民情，又能买到称心如意的商品。

闹市胜景 上海虽是个人口密集的繁华都会，可是闹市中不乏供人们休闲、游览的好去处。如集明清两代江南园林风格的豫园，平均每天接待游客二万人次。江南佛教名刹玉佛寺，在普陀区安远路上，寺内的卧佛堂和玉佛楼供奉从缅甸请回的白玉卧佛和坐像，弥足珍贵。上海近郊、远郊则是一派江南水乡景色，著名的景点有龙华塔和龙华古寺，淀山湖大观园游览区，嘉定的古猗园、秋霞圃，松江的醉白池、方塔园，佘山天主教堂等等。

弄堂情结 近年来上海修建了许多住宅小区。尽管现代化的住宅设施完善，可是许多上海市民依然眷恋着他们住惯了的石库门、小弄堂里的旧居，毕竟旧情难断啊！

人们都说上海人精明干练，擅于精打细算。从他们居家生活的点点滴滴都可看到这一特点。每天早上家庭主妇挎着篮子从弄堂里出来赶早市，她们奔走于各摊位间，寻寻觅觅，货比三家。经过一番精挑细捡、讨价还价后，归来时菜篮子里有新鲜水灵的蔬菜，活蹦活跳的鱼虾，荤素齐备，恰够一家人一天的食用，不会有浪费。

上海人既勇于吸收、借鉴外来文化，又热爱自己的传统、文化。比如，晨曦中有很多老年人、年轻人走出弄堂，在街心花园里、广场上满怀激情地跳着迪斯科。可是平时他们还是钟情于京昆剧、越剧、沪剧、评弹等传统的戏剧、曲艺，百看不厌。每年四月（农历三月）的龙华庙会上，有各种传统风味小吃，精致的手工艺品，还有杂技、武术、气功等表演，赶庙会的市民摩肩接踵，人山人海，可以看出市民阶层心灵深处对传统文化的挚爱。

新世纪的大上海 当日历翻到 90 年代第一春，中国政府向全世界宣布了开发、开放浦东的重大战略决策。浦东新区与上海市区仅一江之隔，面积 522 平方公里。以浦东开发、开放为契机，上海的改革开放进入了一个崭新的阶段。近年来，上海在发生着深刻的变化，浦东新区一系列基础设施如南浦大桥、杨浦大桥、越江隧道、新港区、电厂等已投入使用。陆家嘴金融贸易区、外高桥保税区、金桥出口加工区、张江高科技园区等已粗具规模，初见成效。有识之士预言：浦东的开发，对振兴上海，带动长江三角洲，乃至全国进一步改革开放、经济起飞，将有深远意义和巨大影响。下个世纪浦东将成为金融中心、商贸中心、房地产交易中心、信息中心、物资配运中心。

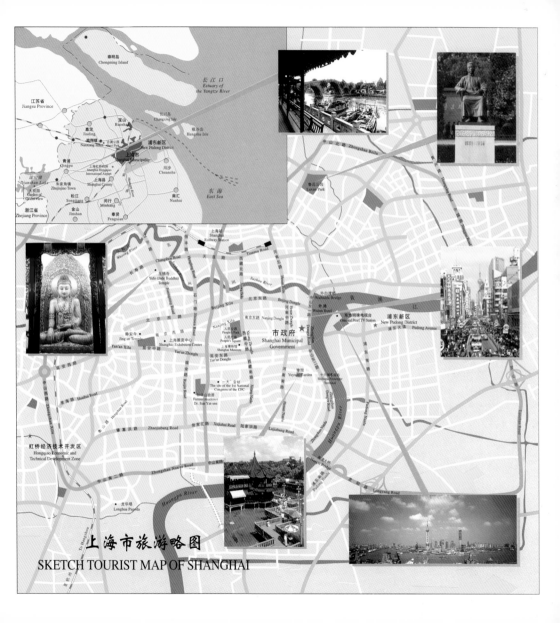

Waitan Bund on the west bank of the Huangpu River, a tributary of the Yangtze River, starts at the confluence of the Suzhou and Huangpu rivers in the north and originally ended at the entrance to Yan'an Donglu in the south. Later the southern end was extended as far as the Nanpu Bridge. In 1843 Shanghai was compelled to open as a trading port. After that, foreign colonialists occupied the prime location that came to be known as Waitan, where they set up commercial firms, banks and consulates. Ships soon crowded the river, and merchants lined its banks; hence, Shanghai became a "paradise for adventurers." Half a century ago the colonialists were driven away, but all these buildings have been well preserved, which may help remind the local people of the past and prod them to look to the future. Upper right: Yulan (magnolia), Shanghai's municipal flower.

外滩位于长江下游支流黄浦江西畔,北起苏州河与黄浦江交汇处,南至延安东路路口,后又向南延伸至南浦大桥。1843 年上海被迫开辟为通商口岸后,外国殖民主义者占有了外滩这段黄金地带,建起各式商厦、银行、领事馆等建筑。一时江上船舶穿梭,岸上商贾云集,这里成了"冒险家的乐园"。半个世纪前,殖民主义者被逐,这些建筑仍完整保存,供人们回忆与思考。右上图为上海市市花白玉兰花。

9

Decoration in an old building on Waitan. Built in English classical style, the building was used as the headquarters of the British Banking Corporation Ltd. The inside of the dome of the building has 33 panels of mosaic pictures. In the 1950s they were painted over, but the new owner of the building, the Pudong Development Bank, removed the paint while renovating the building.

When evening comes, the banks of the Huangpu River are thronged with strolling young couples.

外滩一幢旧建筑中新发现的壁画。这幢具有英国古典风格的建筑曾是英国汇丰银行的营业楼,大楼穹顶有用彩色马赛克镶拼的反映神话故事的33幅壁画。50年代被刷上涂料封存。最近大楼新主人浦东发展银行在修缮施工中使之重现于世。

夜色降临,黄浦江畔是年青人谈情说爱的地方。

Bustling Nanjing Road, 5,400 m long, stretches from Waitan to the entrance to Yan'an Xilu. It is known locally as "Ten-li Street." Many of Shanghai's leading commercial buildings are located here. When evening comes, Nanjing Road shimmers with colorful neon lights.

南京路东起外滩,西至延安西路,全长5400米,号称"十里长街"。许多有名的商厦设立于此。入夜,南京路流光溢彩,火树银花,成了不夜城。

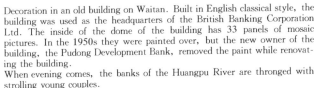

Glimpses of Old Shanghai

① Paomating (race course) was built in 1868. Its site is now People's Square.

② Old Waitan.

③ A scene on Fujian Road, taken in 1915, which was well known for its garment workshops.

旧上海一瞥

①开设于 1868 年的赌场跑马厅，1954 年改建成人民广场。

②昔日外滩

③1915 年时的福建路，曾以成衣业闻名沪上。

The Waibaidu Bridge is where the Suzhou River flows into the Huangpu. This bridge was built with funds collected from foreigners, and so only foreigners could cross it without paying a toll. The name Waibaidu means "foreigners can cross without paying."

苏州河汇入黄浦江处的外白渡桥。因当年是外国人集资兴建，外国人过往免费，中国人无此权利，故厌恶地称之为"外白渡桥"。

A bird's-eye-view of People's Square. Surrounding it are the municipal government office building, the Shanghai Museum and the Opera House; in the center is a musical fountain. The 100-m-wide avenue traverses the square from west to east.

14

鸟瞰上海人民广场。周围楼群有市政府办公大楼、上海博物馆、大歌剧院等。广场中心有巨型音乐喷泉。宽达百米的大道贯穿东西。

15

The newly built Shanghai Museum contains 130,000 objects, including precious bronze and porcelain wares, books and paintings. In the picture on the right is an ancient bronze cauldron on display at the museum.

新建的上海博物馆是一座大型的综合性的艺术博物馆，以收藏青铜器、陶瓷器、书画珍品著称，藏品达 13 万余件。右图为陈列室内景。

The Dashijie (Great World) Recreation Center, which opened in 1917, was a resort for hooligans, prostitutes, gamblers and drug addicts in the old days. After the founding of New China in 1949 it was rebuilt, and contains a dance hall, cinema, roller-skating rink and other recreational facilities.
Below: The newly completed Shanghai Opera House.

大世界游乐中心创办于 1917 年,解放前这里是流氓妓女混杂,赌博吸毒泛滥的场所。解放后改建成市内最早的游乐场,内设舞厅、电影院、溜冰场、游艺宫等。
下图是新落成的上海大歌剧院。

The First National Congress of the Communist Party of China was held in Shanghai in July 1921, at which the birth of the Party was declared. This is the meeting site, 76 Xingye Road (106 Wangzhi Road in the old days).

中国共产党第一次全国代表大会 1921 年 7 月在上海召开,宣告了中国共产党的诞生。图为兴业路 76 号(原望志路 106 号)会址。

No. 7 Xiangshan Road is the former residence of Dr. Sun Yat-sen, a pioneer of the Chinese revolution. He lived there in his later years, making the decision to unite with the CPC and studying a plan to reorganize the Kuomintang.

坐落在香山路 7 号（原莫利爱路 29 号）的孙中山故居。伟大的革命先行者孙中山先生晚年居住在这里。他晚年顺应时代前进的潮流，就在这所房子里确定联共的政策，研究改组国民党的方案。

Soong Ching Ling, wife of Dr. Sun, was a leader of the People's Republic of China, stateswoman and social activist. After 1948 she lived at 1843 Huaihai Zhonglu. Above: A statue of Soong Ching Ling. Below: Her bedroom, furnished as it was in those days.

孙夫人宋庆龄是中华人民共和国的领导人、政治家、社会活动家。她自 1948 年起即寓居于淮海中路 1843 号。上图为宋庆龄坐像。下图为故居卧室,室内陈列物皆是生前原物。

◁ The Jade Buddha Temple is situated on Anyuan Road. The jade statue of Sakyamuni in the picture, 1.9 m high, was brought to the temple by the monk Huigen from Myanmar around 1875 (the first year of Qing Emperor Guangxu's reign).

玉佛寺坐落在安远路上。图为该寺供奉的玉雕释迦牟尼坐像,像高 1.9 米,是僧人慧根于清光绪初年(约 1875 年)由缅甸迎回的。

Longhua Town in the southwestern suburbs is famous for its ancient temple and pagoda. It is said that the Longhua Temple was built in 242 (during the time of the Wu Kingdom of the Three Kingdoms Period). It was destroyed during a war and rebuilt in 977 (during the Song Dynasty). Left: The one-thousand-armed Bodhisattva Guanyin worshipped in the temple. Right: The exquisite seven-storey octagonal Longhua Pagoda, built of bricks and timber.

上海西南郊的龙华镇,以古刹、宝塔而驰名。相传龙华寺建于三国时吴国赤乌五年(242 年),后毁于战乱,宋太平兴国二年(977 年)重建。左图为龙华寺中供奉的千手观音菩萨。右图为砖木结构的龙华塔,七层八角,玲珑秀丽。

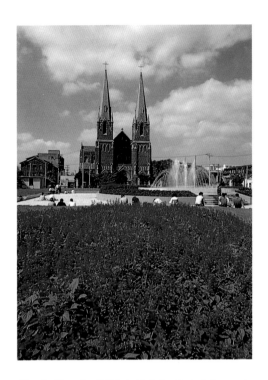

24

The Gothic-style Xujiahui Catholic Cathedral — the largest Catholic place of worship in Shanghai.

这座中世纪哥特式建筑为上海地区最大的天主教堂——徐家汇天主教堂。

The International Church, situated at the intersection of ▷ Hengshan and Urumqi roads.

位于衡山路与乌鲁木齐路相交处的国际礼拜堂内景。

A bird's-eye-view of the old Chenghuangmiao Temple area. The temple, at 249 Fangbang Zhonglu, is a Taoist one. In the old days temple fairs were held here on special days. Gradually the permanent temple market was formed, encompassing the Yuyuan Garden and the Zigzag Bridge. There is an authentic local flavor about this busy market area, where the locals have preserved their unique life styles and customs.

鸟瞰老城隍庙一带建筑群。老城隍庙位于方浜中路 249 号，是一处道教圣迹。过去庙会盛行，香客不断，庙内外云集了许多小吃摊、百货摊和杂耍摊，逐渐形成以豫园九曲桥为中心的庙会市场。这里的民居、弄堂、商铺自成格局。这一带的居民多是上海的老市民，风情、习俗饶有特色。

The Zigzag Bridge is one of the scenic spots in the downtown part of Shanghai. The ▷ bridge was originally part of the Yuyuan Garden, but is now outside it.

豫园九曲桥，可谓闹市中一景。原是豫园园内建筑的一部分，现已独立于外。

The Yuyuan Garden, adjoining the Chenghuangmiao Temple, was built in 1559. The huge garden boasts 48 unique scenic spots.

豫园建于 1559 年, 与老城隍庙毗连。园中置景 48 处, 园中套园, 千姿百态。

28

① The Yangshan Hall, from the top of which one gets a fine view of the artificial hill across the pond.
② The tranquil Yuhua Hall was originally the master of the house's study.
③ This exquisite lump of jade came from Lake Taihu. It is said to have been intended as a gift for Emperor Huizong of the Song Dynasty, over 1,000 years ago. It is now located in front of the Yuhua Hall.
④ This is the Moonbeam-Basking Building. Its name is taken from the saying, "Buildings at the water's edge get the moonlight first."

①造型别致的仰山堂,登楼观望,可见对面一池相隔的假山。
②玉华堂,原为园主人书斋,环境幽静。
③玉华堂前的太湖石玉玲珑,据说是宋徽宗收集天下奇石时的遗物,已有千年历史。
④临水而筑的得月楼,楼名取"近水楼台先得月"之意。

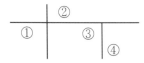

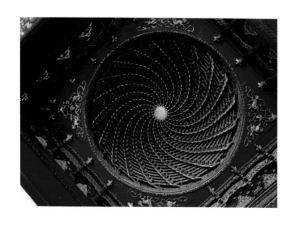

The stage in the Yuyuan Garden is the oldest and best-preserved stage in Shanghai. The picture above is of the caisson ceiling of the stage.

豫园大戏台,是豫园古建筑中的精品,也是上海现存最古老、保存最完整的戏台。上图为大戏台藻井,雕梁画栋,古画盎然。

These photographs of Pudong taken from the west bank of the Huangpu River at the end of the 1980s and in November 1997, respectively, show the great changes that have taken place in Pudong.

由黄浦江西岸望浦东。两幅照片，分别摄于 80 年代末和 1997 年 11 月，从中可以看到浦东的巨变。

Shanghai's traffic congestion has been greatly alleviated in recent years through a series of construction projects. Right: The newly built 48-km elevated Inner Ring Road. Left: The Xujiahui Station of the No. 1 Subway Line. The line is 16.1 km long, and the station is the largest subway station in Asia.

经过近年来的改造和建设,上海的交通拥挤状况已有改观。右图为近年兴建的内环线高架公路,全长 48 公里。左图为地铁一号线上亚洲最大的地铁站徐家汇站。地铁一号线全长 16.1 公里。

In order to expedite the development of Pudong, three bridges have been built over the Huangpu River to connect it with downtown Shanghai. The picture on the left shows the Nanpu Bridge; top right is the Yangpu Bridge; lower right is the newly built Xupu Bridge.

为开发浦东,在黄浦江上已建成三座大桥,沟通了浦江两岸。左为南浦大桥,右上为杨浦大桥,右下为新建成的徐浦大桥。

Shanghai at Night

① Illuminated buildings on Waitan reflected in the river.
② The Oriental Pearl — Shanghai's radio and TV tower — soars into the sky from the east bank of the Huangpu River.
③ Night at Huanqiu Leyuan (Global Paradise).
④ The Hongqiao Economic and Technical Development Zone at night.

夜上海景观

①流光溢彩的外滩建筑群倒映在浦江中
②矗立在浦东的东方明珠广播电视塔
③环球乐园里的欢乐之夜
④夜色中的虹桥经济技术开发区

The Nanshi District in the south of the city, also called the old city district, was Shanghai's first residential district. The picture was taken before the recent renovation of the area. The picture on the right shows the balcony of a house on Changli Road, where a retired worker enjoys growing flowers and keeping pet birds.

位于城南的南市区是上海最早的居民区,俗称老城厢。这里街道狭窄住宅密集。如今,这一带的旧宅已拆除,正在重建,图为拆除前的旧观。右上为昌里路上一处民宅的阳台,一方不足十平米的小天地里,有鸟笼,有盆花,这位退休老人乐在其中。

These houses exhibit the typical Shanghai style of the 1920s. Many artists and writers of the time lived in such cramped dwellings.

石库门住宅，是具有 20 年代上海地方风格的民居建筑。其外观整齐划一，内部结构却局促、狭小。这种住宅往往在楼层之间延伸出一间小屋，俗称亭子间，只能摆下一床一桌。因为房租便宜，过去一些贫穷的文人、作家常租住这种房子。石库门里既居住过芸芸众生，也孕育过众多的名人哲士。

44

Upper left: Huile Lane off Fuzhou Road used to be a red light district. In the 1950s the lane became a residential area. It was razed in 1996 to make way for up-to-date dwellings.
Lower right: An old house on Changsheng Street in the Nanshi District.

左上：位于福州路的会乐里，这里曾是旧上海妓院集中的地方。50 年代后成为市民居住的里弄。已于 1996 年拆除，将在这里重建新住宅楼。
右下图，南市区长生街一所老宅。

The best-preserved house in the typical south-China style is this one in Lujiazui in the New Pudong District. The decoration on the door, windows and veranda posts are patterned on ancient Chinese wood-cut designs.

浦东新区陆家嘴保存最完整的一座江南民居。院内门窗、廊柱上的纹饰由法国传统的百合花纹和中国古老的木雕图案组合而成，具有东西融合的建筑风格。

46

Shanghai's chequered history is reflected in the mixture of architectural styles to be found all over the city. Buildings typical of many countries stand cheek by jowl with modern Chinese structures.

由于历史的原因，上海拥有世界上各种风格的建筑，因而有"万国建筑博物馆"之誉。一些保留下来的具有异国特色的旧建筑与近年新建的楼群错落相间，构成了上海特有的风貌。

The old southern-style buildings are splendidly decorated and ingeniously constructed.

上海的旧式建筑装饰华丽,结构繁巧,具有江南传统风格。

48

Shanghai, known as a "shopper's paradise," has a great number of renowned shops stocked with large numbers of exquisite commodities. Left: The old Chenghuangmiao market, or Yuyuan Market, well known for offering small commodities in more varieties than any other market in the country. Upper right: The interior of a porcelain ware shop on Nanjing Xilu.

上海有"购物天堂"之称,名店林立,精品荟萃。左图为老城隍庙商场(又称豫园商场),以专营特色小商品著称,其品种之多、之全为全国之最。右上图是南京西路上的瓷器专卖店。

Shanghai's snacks are renowned all over China for their ingenuity and variety. Left: Nanxiang stuffed buns cooked in bamboo steamers. Below: A teahouse in a pondside pavilion. The local people drink tea, chat and enjoy the scenery here on fine days.

上海的小吃以制作精制、品种繁多而闻名全国。左图为有名小吃南翔小笼包子。下图为湖心亭茶室，人们可在此品茗、赏景、谈心。

53

Left: Temple fair on a festive occasion. Right: Ceremonial music dating from the time of Confucius is played at the temple fair.

左图是节日庙会的盛况。右图为演奏古老的孔乐舞曲。

Abacuses of every description, collected by Chen Baoding. Collections kept by individuals in Shanghai account for 50 percent of those in the whole country.

上海的民间收藏占中国个人收藏的 50％，有"半壁江山"之誉。图为"算盘大王"陈宝定收藏的各式各样的算盘。

The Shanghai Acrobatic Troupe is one of the leading ▷ companies of its kind in China.

上海杂技团正在演出。

56

Many types of opera and folk art are popular in Shanghai, especially Suzhou Pingtan (story telling and ballad singing in the Suzhou dialect, above). Right: A scene from the Kunqu opera *Zhong Kui Marries Off His Sister*.

上海流行的戏剧曲艺丰富多彩，用吴语演唱的苏州评弹尤受市民喜爱。上图为评弹演出时情景。右图是昆剧《钟馗嫁妹》中的一个场面。

The Fan Dance is both a recreational activity and a form of physical exercise. Different from the Yangge Dance popular in the north, it is marked by lithe movements in the southern dance style.

上海人喜爱的文娱、体育活动——扇舞，它不同于北方的扭秧歌，富有江南柔美的风格。

There is no shortage of interesting things to do for young people in Shanghai.

都市青年人的生活别有一番情趣。

The Square Pagoda of Songjiang is located in the Xingshengjiao Temple, which dates from 949. The pagoda was built in the period 1068 to 1094 during the Northern Song Dynasty. The nine-storey square pagoda is 48.5 m high. Upper right: A brick pagoda in Jiading County, which dates from the early years of the Northern Song Dynasty (960-1127).

兴圣教寺塔,即松江方塔。寺建于五代后汉乾佑二年(949年),北宋熙宁至元佑年间(1068 - 1094 年)造塔。塔为砖木结构,九级方形,总高 48.5 米。右上图为嘉定砖塔,始建于五代至北宋初年,已有 1000 多年历史。

60

The Guyi Park, situated in Nanxiang Town, Jiading County, was built in the Wanli reign period (1573 to 1619) of the Ming Dynasty and renovated in the Qing Dynasty (1644-1911). The garden, in which are preserved many cultural relics of the Tang, Song, Ming and Qing dynasties (618-1911), is one of the most famous classical gardens of Shanghai.

古猗园位于嘉定县南翔镇,明万历年间(1573－1619年)建造,清代重新修葺。园内保存有唐、宋、明、清历代文物,是沪上著名古典园林之一。

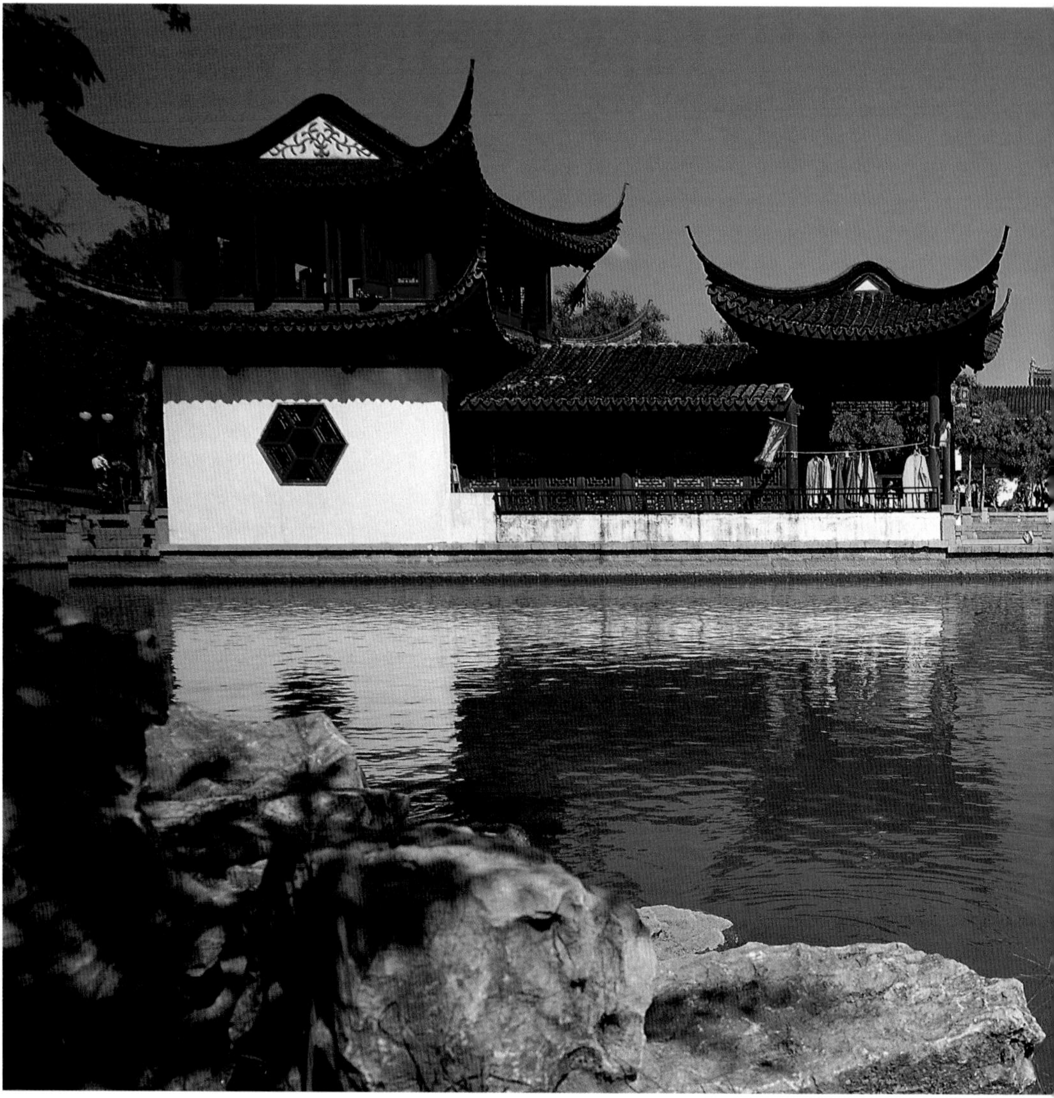

The Garden of Grand View Resort, situated beside Dian-shan Lake, Qingpu County, covers eight ha and has 8,000 sq m of building area. The buildings and the layout of the garden reproduce the garden of the same name in the classical novel *A Dream of Red Mansions*.

大观园游览区位于青浦淀山湖畔,占地 8 公顷多,建筑面积 8000 多平方米。园中建筑、布局是参照古典小说《红楼梦》中描述的大观园建造、配置的。

A traditional wedding ceremony performed in the Villa of Visiting Parents.
① Performing the formal wedding ceremony.
② The bridegroom leads the bride to the bridal chamber.

省亲别墅内的婚俗表演。①拜堂 ②入洞房

◁ The Villa of Visiting Parents is the main building in the Garden of Grand View.

"省亲别墅"是大观园中的主要建筑。

A panorama of the Garden of Grand View, which embodies the features of both imperial and private gardens in ancient China.

大观园全景。它集皇家御苑和私家园林之长，兼有雍容华贵与古朴典雅之趣。

68

The Fangsheng (Freeing Captive Creatures) Bridge, east of Zhujiajiao Town in Qingpu County, has five arches. It was built with money raised by monks in the fifth year of the Longqing reign period (1571) of the Ming Dynasty. The bridge got its name because under it fish and turtles are freed and allowed to live undisturbed. Freeing captured creatures is an act of piety in the Buddhist religion.

放生桥位于青浦古镇朱家角镇东，为五孔联拱石桥。明隆庆五年(1571年)由寺僧募款建造，并规定桥下只许放生鱼鳖，不准捕捞，故名放生桥。

The old street of Shipijie in Zhujiajiao is so narrow that the people living on the top floors can pass things from one to the other over the street.

古镇朱家角的一条老街,旧称石皮街。街道窄狭,街两边的楼上人家可以伸手相互递物。

Folk paintings of Jinshan County, a south China folk painting genre, are done by female peasants skilled in embroidery and weaving. These paintings are specialties of the Jinshan Peasant Art Academy.

金山农民画。它是江南民间绘画艺术中的一个流派，作者多为能绣善织的农妇。她们还组织了"金山农民画院"。

The suburbs of Shanghai are a patchwork of rivers and lakes. In spring the land is green and fragrant with flowers. This is a time when Shanghai residents make excursions into the countryside which surrounds their bustling metropolis. Upper right: An old-fashioned waterwheel. People from the city like to have a try at it to experience what life used to be like in the countryside. Below: Young people flying kites in the fields.

上海郊区是水乡平原，入春后遍地春色，花香四溢，人们走出喧闹的市区尽情享受大自然的乐趣。右上图脚踩水车原是一种古老的汲水灌溉工具。如今成了供城里人体验农耕辛乐的设施。下图是在田野里放风筝的孩子们。

图书在版编目(CIP)数据

上海:英汉/兰佩瑾编。- 北京:外文出版社,1998
ISBN 7-119-02221-0

Ⅰ.上…Ⅱ.兰…Ⅲ.摄影集-中国-上海 Ⅳ.J426.51
中国版本图书馆 CIP 数据核字(98)第 15631 号

Edited by: Lan Peijin
Text by: Yang Shijin   Wu Wen
Photos by: Xie Xinfa   Da Xiangqun
Yang Zhongjian   Chen Kejia
Lan Peijin
Translated by: Cai Guanping
Designed by: Yuan Qing

First Edition   1999
Ninth Printing   2006

Shanghai

ISBN 7-119-02221-0

© Foreign Languages Press
Published by Foreign Languages Press
24 Baiwanzhuang Road, Beijing 100037, China
Home Page: http://www.flp.com.cn
E-mail Addresses: info @ flp.com.cn
sales @ flp.com.cn
Printed in the People's Republic of China

编辑: 兰佩瑾
撰文: 杨时进   吴 文
摄影: 谢新发   达向群
杨中俭   陈克家
兰佩瑾等
翻译: 蔡关平
设计: 元 青

上 海

兰佩瑾 编

© 外文出版社
外文出版社出版
(中国北京百万庄大街 24 号)
邮政编码 100037
外文出版社网页: http://www.flp.com.cn
外文出版社电子邮件地址: info @ flp.com.cn
sales @ flp.com.cn
北京京都六环印刷厂
1999 年(24 开)第一版
2006 年第一版第九次印刷
(英汉)
ISBN 7-119-02221-0
04800 (精)